How Animals Survive

By Ross E. Hutchins

Photographs by the author

FINDING-OUT BOOKS

Parents' Magazine Press · New York

Library of Congress Cataloging in Publication Data

Hutchins, Ross E.
   How animals survive.

   (Finding-out books)
   SUMMARY: Describes how animals survive by using
their armor, camouflage, horns, stings, and other
natural protective devices.
   1. Animal defenses—Juvenile literature.
[1. Animal defenses]   I. Title.

QL759.H85   591.5'7   73-15692
ISBN 0-8193-0754-8

Contents

INTRODUCTION

Animals have many ways of staying alive in a world where competition is keen. These include such protection as hard body armor, horns, and poison stings.

No creature lives for long in the world unless it can protect itself from enemies and obtain food. In nature there are always the hunters and the hunted. Those that feed on plants are almost always in danger from flesh eaters. But the flesh eaters, in turn, must protect themselves from other flesh eaters.

Animals living today are those that have been successful in the struggle for survival that has been going on for millions of years. They have survived because they are a little better fitted for the lives they live. Scientists keep finding remains, or *fossils*, of animals that died out long ago. These are the ones left along the trail of time because they could not compete in the struggle. For example, the great dinosaurs passed out of the picture a long time ago. We are not sure why. Perhaps climates became too cold for them and, since they were cold-blooded and could not change, they died out, or became extinct.

In this book you will read about modern animals that do stay alive and the kinds of natural protection they have which make it possible.

1. ANIMALS IN ARMOR

Armored ships and tanks have been used in warfare by humans for many years. Knights wore suits of mail as a defense against spears and arrows. Before that, men protected themselves in battle with shields made of animal skins and wood. Yet the use of armor is not a man-made method of protection by any means. Animals—and some plants—have been using body armor for millions of years. For instance, tiny plants, living in the sea, called *diatomes*, have shells made of silicon, which is found in sand and glass. Diatomes are very old; it is known that they lived in the world's most ancient seas many millions of years ago.

Much later, armored fish lived in these same seas. Their armor was a protection against such enemies as sharks, whose jaws were set with rows of teeth almost as hard and sharp as steel. Competition for food was keen and so only the strongest creatures that lived in the sea were able to survive. Some of these ancient fish were protected by plate-like scales, which some modern fish still have.

In time, fresh-water streams and lakes became populated by fish of many kinds including the sturgeon and the gar, both of which have plate-like scales. The bodies of gars, especially, are covered with scales that are almost as

The scales of the gar.

hard as stone and are set closely together like chain mail. Gar fish are still common in the rivers and lakes of the southeastern United States, where they often grow very large. Some, such as the alligator gar, may grow to 10 feet in length and weigh 400 pounds. So hard are the scales of a large gar that a 22-caliber rifle bullet can't dent them. These scales are roughly arrow-shaped and are set closely together in a pattern that looks almost like the tile in our bathrooms. Indians sometimes used these hard scales instead

When seen separately, gar scales look like arrowheads.

of flint for arrowheads. Because of their hard body armor, gars have few natural enemies. Instead, they are the enemies of other fish, which they capture in their powerful jaws set with rows of needle-like teeth.

Many land animals, too, have body armor that protects them. There are many examples. We immediately think of reptiles such as turtles, snakes, lizards, and alligators. All these creatures have scale-covered bodies. Notice how much a turtle resembles an armored tank. Both upper and lower portions of its body are covered with hard plate-like scales that are attached to the animal's inner skeleton. The body of a turtle is like a box, giving the animal good protection against most enemies. Both head and legs, in most cases, may be drawn into the shell-like case. In the common box

7

The common box turtle looks like a tank.

turtle, the bottom portion of the shell is hinged front and back and may be tightly closed after the head, legs, and tail are drawn inside. After these "doors" are closed, it is almost impossible for an enemy to harm the turtle in its fortress. In some cases, however, one of these small turtles may become very fat. Then it cannot close its shell completely. This leaves the little creature at the mercy of enemies.

There are many kinds of turtles—from giant sea turtles down to tiny pond turtles. The largest fresh-water turtle native to North America is probably the alligator snapping turtle. These turtles sometimes grow to large size, weighing more than 200 pounds. They are armored with large, hard, plate-like scales and have powerful cutting jaws that could easily cut a man's arm off. Needless to say, they have few natural enemies.

Most other reptiles are not as well protected as the turtles. The bodies of snakes, lizards, and alligators are covered with scales. Since these scales are attached to the skin, their

Like all reptiles, the body of the alligator is protected by heavy plates and scales. It also has powerful jaws and sharp teeth.

The armadillo is one of the few warm-blooded animals that have bodies protected by scales and plates.

bodies are flexible, allowing for free and rapid movement. This helps them to escape from enemies.

Some mammals, which are warm-blooded animals usually covered with hair, also have body armor. The armadillo is probably the best example. Most of the upper portion of an armadillo's body is covered with hard, scale-like plates that must help to keep it safe. These creatures have nothing but their hard covering to use as defense. When alarmed, an armadillo often curls its body up into a ball. This protects its soft underparts from harm.

From fossils found in North and South America we know that about 100 million years ago there were giant armadillos as long as 15 feet. These strange armored mammals ranged only as far north as Texas.

Even more remarkable than the armadillos are their relatives, the pangolins, the largest of which is the giant pangolin of Africa, which weighs up to 60 pounds and is 6 feet long. Its body is covered with large plates. When curled up in its protective pose, it resembles a large pine cone. It has a yard-long tongue used to capture ants.

Of all the world's creatures with body armor that protects them, the largest group is the Arthropods—joint-legged animals. Crabs, lobsters, crayfish, and insects all belong to this group. All these animals have *exo-skeletons*. That is, their skeletons are on the outside, forming a hard covering or shell.

The next time you see a large beetle, notice how much it looks like a steel-covered tank. Its shell is very hard and

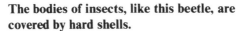

The bodies of insects, like this beetle, are covered by hard shells.

its legs are hinged, with few places where an enemy could injure it. Perhaps the best example to study is a large male rhinoceros beetle. It has a heavy spine or horn on the top of its body, just back of the head, known as the *prothorax*. These large beetles are often attracted to lights. They weigh more than an ounce, have very powerful legs, and can also fly easily. They have few enemies because most birds would not be able to break through their hard shells.

Before it is fully grown, when it is in what is called the grub stage, a rhinoceros beetle lives in a rotten log. At this time its body is soft and white and almost any creature could eat it. But deep in the rotting wood of its log, where it stays, it is safe. When it changes into a beetle and leaves the rotting log to mate, it is faced with many enemies and must be protected if it is to live. Thus, millions of years ago, it got its hard shell.

The body walls of insects are made up of three layers. The two inner ones contain a very hard substance called *chitin* (pronounced ky-tin). Chitin cannot be dissolved by most liquids. It cannot be digested by animals. The body covering of insects and similar creatures, looks, in a way, like the armor worn by medieval knights and serves more or less the same purpose.

Like insects, the bodies of crabs, lobsters, and crayfish are enclosed in hard shells. These give excellent protection that has allowed them to survive for so long.

The bodies of crabs, too, are enclosed in hard shells. This is a fiddler crab, common along many beaches.

Hermit crabs get extra protection by living in abandoned sea snail shells. They crawl about, dragging the heavy shells.

How better could an animal protect itself than by surrounding its body with stone? Millions of years ago, molluscs, such as clams, oysters, and snails got this type of body armor. Otherwise such animals would long ago have died out, or become extinct. No animal survives in the world unless its means of self-protection is efficient.

About 300 million years ago the molluscs became abundant in the ancient seas. They were soft-bodied animals that were protected by shells formed mostly of calcium, the same mineral that limestone is made of. Modern clams, mussels, oysters, and snails came from these ancient molluscs. Most of them have limestone shells.

The common clam is an example of this animal group. It is soft-bodied but encloses itself between two shells, or *valves*, that are hinged at the back and which may be tightly closed by means of powerful muscles. Some clams move about by means of a "foot" that can be pushed out of the

The hard shells of clams give good protection from most enemies. These are scallop shells.

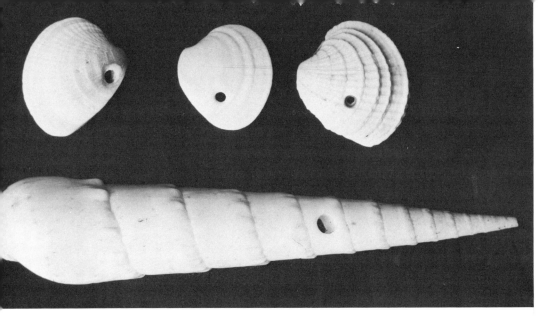

The holes in the shells of these sea clams and snails were made by the oyster drill.

open shell. If anything happens to disturb the clam, the muscles quickly pull the two valves together very tightly. With the animal's body protected between the two stone-like valves, very little harm could come to it.

Oysters are very much like clams except that they anchor themselves in one place, never moving about.

Clams and clam-like animals vary greatly in size. The world's largest is the giant clam of the Indian and South Pacific oceans, which may measure more than 4 feet long and weigh over 400 pounds. Divers have sometimes been drowned by having a foot trapped in a shell that snapped shut upon it. I almost had such an experience myself while skin-diving over a tropical coral reef.

14

The hard shells of clams and oysters protect these animals from most enemies. Anyone who has ever tried to open a clam or an oyster knows this. However, no matter how strong the defense of one animal may be, some other animal can usually find a way around it. If you have ever collected seashells along a beach you have probably found many oyster or clam shells with holes in them. The holes were made by oyster drills. These are sea snails that use their file-like tongues to drill holes into the shells of clams and oysters in order to eat them. Starfish, too, have a way to eat clams. These creatures have many suction feet which they attach to clam shells, gradually forcing them open in order to eat the clam that is inside the shells.

In spite of several important enemies, oysters and clams have survived for millions of years, protected by their heavy limestone shells.

Snails, too, live inside limestone shells that are often very

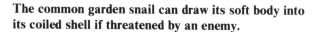

The common garden snail can draw its soft body into its coiled shell if threatened by an enemy.

hard and heavy. Many kinds are found in the sea and in fresh water. Others, long ago, took up life on dry land. A snail pushes its soft body out of its spiral shell and crawls about, feeding. At the first sign of danger it withdraws into its coiled fortress.

Some sea snails grow to large size. The queen conch, for example, may be a foot long. Its shell is beautiful mother-of-pearl.

So, as you can see, man did not invent tanks and body armor; he just copied defense methods that have been used by animals for millions of years.

2. STINGS, POISONS, AND GASES

Human beings have many ways of defending themselves and destroying their enemies. Years and years ago, men often used poison-tipped spears or arrows in tribal battles. During World War I, a new and terrible type of chemical warfare was introduced. This was poison gas. But chemical warfare is not a new method of defense by any means. Like body armor, it has been used by many creatures for a long time as a way of destroying or driving off enemies.

The skunk has one of the most effective defense methods used by any animal.

The best-known type of chemical warfare among animals is the one used by the skunk, a very successful way of getting rid of enemies. That is why a skunk can go in search of food without fear. Only a few natural enemies dare to bother it. One of these is the great horned owl. Dogs sometimes attack skunks, much to their sorrow. Human beings, with their traps and guns, are the skunk's chief enemies.

The skunk's method of defense is so effective that it does not need brains to outwit its enemies.

The scent glands of a skunk are under its tail, one on each side of the rectal opening. When an enemy comes near, a skunk first gives warning by patting its front feet. If the enemy is so foolish as to stay close by, the skunk then turns about, lifts its bushy tail, and fires its stream of scent, often as far as 10 feet. Few animals are able to stand

17

the strong smell and so the skunk goes on its way unharmed. So strong is this scent that many animals, including human beings, are sickened by it. If this stream is fired into a person's eyes, the result may be serious.

So effective is the skunk's method of defense that one wonders why many other creatures do not have it. A few have. One of these is the insect with the common name stink bug. These are medium-sized insects that suck out the sap of plants, sometimes causing damage to them. When handled or placed in the mouth their odor or taste is most disagreeable. I once accidentally placed some blackberries in my mouth and found that there was a stink bug among them. I was careful from then on to look more carefully at the berries before I ate them.

In the United States there is a beetle with a defense somewhat like that of the skunk. These are commonly known as bombardier beetles. They are often found hiding under stones. When disturbed, they let out, with popping

The bombardier beetle lives under rocks or dead bark.

Skull of a cottonmouth moccasin. Notice how the fangs are hinged so that they may be swung forward. The fangs are hollow and the venom is injected through them.

sounds, small smoke-like puffs of irritant gas. No doubt this gas has the effect of driving off enemies.

Poison darts, spears, and arrows, as we have said, were once used by many people in hunting and in warfare. This is a most effective means of offense and defense so it is no surprise that many animals, too, are protected by this kind of chemical defense. You will probably think right away of poisonous snakes and their venom. Snakes of some kinds, such as the cobra, are among the world's most deadly creatures.

We have, in the United States, four types of poisonous snakes: rattlesnakes, moccasins, copperheads, and coral snakes. A bite by a large rattlesnake is, indeed, a most serious and dangerous experience. A rattler's poison glands

19

are located in the head, and small ducts, or tubes, lead from these glands through the hollow fangs, which are folded in the roof of the mouth when the mouth is closed. In the act of striking, a rattler opens its mouth, causing the fangs to swing downward and forward. In this position the fangs can be driven into an enemy and the venom injected, the way a doctor uses a hypodermic needle when he gives you a 'flu shot, for example.

It must be said for the rattlesnake, however, that it usually gives warning with its rattles before striking. If any animal, including man, has injured a rattlesnake by stepping on it, the snake cannot use its venom as defense. So the enemy must be warned away, before it comes too close, and that is the reason for the rattles.

Diamond-back rattlesnake

Scorpion

Many poisonous creatures have ways of frightening enemies away by means of warning sounds or their bright colors that are easily recognized.

Unfortunately, not all poisonous creatures give warning before striking. The scorpion is an example. These dull-colored relatives of insects live in desert regions or under the bark of dead trees in other parts of the United States. If one of them is picked up, it swings its poison-tipped tail forward over its back and plunges its needle-like sting into the hand. The result may be very painful or even result in death in the case of some Mexican species. Thus scorpions are usually treated with respect. Or, better still, let alone.

**Hornets, wasps, and bees have their stings in
their tails. This is a wasp's tail.**

Little need be said about the stings of wasps and bees.
We are all familiar with them and keep away from them
when we can. The stings of these insects are located in the
tail and there are poison or venom glands nearby. When
disturbed, a bee or wasp drives its sharp sting into the flesh
of its attacker and injects a tiny amount of venom. This
causes great pain and, later, swelling.

Almost everyone avoids close contact with bees and
wasps and so these insects go about their business
unharmed.

Many caterpillars, too, have ways of protecting themselves with poisons. It is well to avoid contact with almost any colorful, spiny caterpillar. The needle-like spines of many kinds are filled with powerful venom. Many of these caterpillars have colorful markings that warn enemies away. The green, spiny caterpillar of the io moth is easily recognized and thus can be avoided. So are the colorful little saddle-back caterpillars that are bright green with orange, saddle-like markings on their backs. However, not all caterpillars have warning colors. For example, puss-moth

Most poisonous caterpillars, such as this slug caterpillar, are brightly colored.

caterpillars are covered with brownish fur. This soft fur hides many poison spines. Let them alone!

Among spiders we find several whose bites are dangerous. The most important of these is the well-known black widow. Like some poisonous caterpillars, it has a warning color, being jet-black with a red hour-glass marking on the underside of its abdomen.

These have been a few examples of the many creatures that defend themselves with poisonous chemicals or venoms.

A black widow spider with her egg sac.

The hawk is a keen-eyed hunter. Its beak is well fitted for catching prey and for tearing flesh.

3. JAWS, CLAWS, AND TEETH

An animal that lives by hunting other creatures usually has sharp teeth and claws. The lion and the tiger are among the best examples, but there are many others.

Hawks and eagles live on birds, rats, mice, and other creatures. These birds have sharp curved beaks and talons with which they capture their food. In addition, they have keener eyesight than any other creatures.

On the ground, members of the cat and dog family also live by the hunt. The mountain lion or panther, now found mostly in the western United States, may be as much as 9 feet long and weigh nearly 300 pounds. Such an animal may easily kill a large buck deer.

The bobcat is another member of the cat family still found in most parts of our country. These animals often weigh up to 25 pounds. They are true hunters, feeding on rabbits, squirrels, rats, mice, and birds. Their weapons, like those of the bigger cats, are fangs, claws, and speed. Their chief enemies are human beings.

Closely related to the domestic dog are the wolves, coyotes, and foxes. All these animals are hunters, living by preying on other creatures, especially those smaller than they are. Unlike the cat family, these wild dogs do not depend much on claws; their weapons are their teeth and their cunning. The teeth of a wolf fit so tightly together that they are able to cut flesh or bone like a cleaver. All these animals have large, sharp, canine, or tearing, teeth, used for seizing and holding prey.

The gray fox

Smaller than the wolf is the coyote, the wild dog of the Great Plains and western mountains. Like the wolf, the coyote is a hunter, preying on rabbits, prairie dogs, or, sometimes, deer. However, a coyote will not turn up its nose at game killed by other hunting animals. The coyote was hated by cattlemen and ranchers because it killed sheep and calves. They thought the coyote one of the cleverest of the local wild animals.

The teeth of several animals deserve special mention. Usually we can easily guess an animal's food habits by examining its teeth. The teeth of bats and shrews are slender and needle-like, well fitted for capturing and eating insects. The teeth of deer, cattle, and horses are designed for grinding up the plants they feed on. The chisel-like front teeth of rodents such as rats, mice, muskrats, and beaver are fitted for gnawing hard objects.

Probably the most remarkable of all rodent teeth are

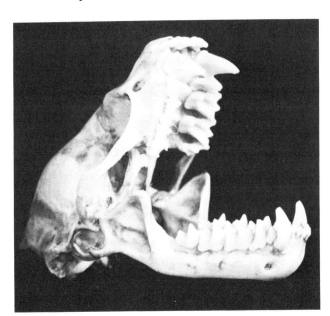

Skull of a bat. Notice the sharp teeth.

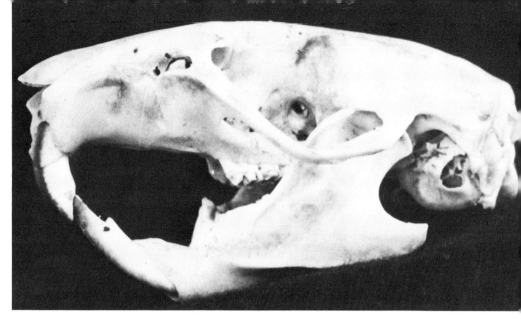

Notice the chisel-like front teeth of this rat skull.

those of the beaver. A beaver's front teeth are very large, with keen cutting edges. The front edges of these teeth are much harder than the rear portions. Thus, they remain sharp as they wear away. Also, these front teeth grow throughout life. It is by means of these teeth that beavers cut down large trees for the building of their dams and stick houses. A beaver can cut down a 5-inch tree in about ten minutes. Beavers have been known to cut down trees with trunks as large as 38 inches across.

The jaws of insects are used not only to capture prey but as tools. With these tools they build nests, dig in the earth, cut through hard wood, and care for their young. The paper-making hornet uses its sharp jaws to gather wood fiber which it then makes into paper for covering its nest. Honeybees use their jaws to build wax cells in which food is stored and young are reared.

The harvester ant has sharp, powerful jaws.

Perhaps the most remarkable of all wasps is the *Ammophila* that, after closing her nest tunnel in the ground, picks up a small pebble in her jaws and uses it to hammer down the sand over the nest opening. It was thus the first creature to use a "tool."

Ants use their jaws for almost everything they do. Harvester ants gather seeds, using their jaws to carry them into their underground nests. In the nest are worker ants of a special type, having very large jaws. These, sometimes called millers, use their jaws to cut up the hard seeds so that the other ants may feed on them.

In Central and South America are found the famous army ants that stream through the jungles in vast numbers,

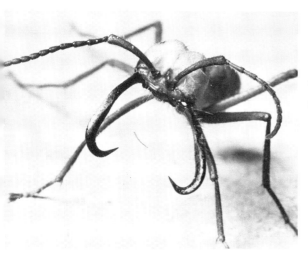

The army ant. These ants are blind.

capturing and eating almost any small creature in their path. The jaws of these ants look like slender ice tongs. They use their jaws to capture prey, carry their young, and defend themselves. They have no permanent homes. They move from place to place, always seeking prey.

Similar ants occur in Africa. These are the driver ants. Like their cousins, the army ants, these ants are always on the hunt for food and they will attack almost any creature, no matter how large, especially if it cannot escape. There is on record a case in which a full-grown leopard was killed while in a cage. Its bones were picked clean in a single night by these voracious ants.

The large soldier of the African driver ants. The small ant at the left is a small worker.

The male elk has spreading antlers. (Courtesy, Denver Museum of Natural History.)

4. HORNS, ANTLERS, AND SPINES

Horns and antlers are used for two things: for fighting between males and for defense against enemies. While horns and antlers seem to be much alike, they are quite different. A horn has two layers: an inner one that is really part of the skull, and an outer, horny layer, which comes from the skin. Blood circulates between these two layers. Horns are not shed each year.

Antlers, on the other hand, come mostly from the skin. In most cases only the male deer, or bucks, have antlers. They begin growing in spring and by late summer are fully formed. During the summer, however, they are soft and are

31

**Elk in early summer when their antlers
are "in the velvet."**

spoken of as being "in the velvet." When injured, they
bleed. In late summer the blood vessels dry up and the dead
skin begins to peel off, often hanging in tatters. At this
season the bucks polish their antlers by rubbing them
against bushes and small trees to get ready for the fall
mating season when the bucks fight each other over the
females, or does. After the mating season, the antlers are
shed. They simply drop off, one by one.

There are many kinds of deer, including the elk, the
moose, and the reindeer, or caribou, all of which belong
to the deer family. The female reindeer has antlers. Each
kind has its own type of antler. Those of the moose, for
example, are broad and flat with many points. Only two
kinds of deer do not have antlers. These are the musk deer

of Asia and the Chinese water deer. Instead of antlers these deer have long canine teeth which they use in battle.

Deer of one kind or another are found in almost all parts of the United States. In addition to antlers as weapons, they have very sharp, cutting hoofs. So-called tame deer have often turned on their owners and killed or injured them by striking with their front hoofs.

Goats, sheep, buffalo, and cattle have true horns. The same is also true of many of the grazing animals of South Africa, including the gnu or wildebeest. Africa has more members of the cattle family than any other continent.

Native to North America are such "cattle" as mountain sheep, mountain goats, bison or buffalo, and the muskox.

The buffalo or bison belongs to the cattle family and has true horns. In the background are two elk.

As we have said, all these members of the cattle family have true horns that are never shed. Not only are they used by the males in fighting with other males but in defense as well. Sharp horns are effective weapons, indeed. They serve their owners well and help them survive in lands where there are many great cats, such as tigers, lions, and panthers. The African water buffalo, for example, is one of the world's most feared beasts.

Though not of the deer and cattle families, the African rhinoceros also has horns—a long, sharp horn in front and a shorter horn behind, both located on its nose. A rhinoceros horn, however, is different from most other horns. It arises from the skin and consists of a mass of hair-like fibers growing solidly together. It is, of course, very hard. The rhinoceros uses its sharp horns in defense in a very effective fashion. The rhinoceros of India has only one horn on its nose which is short and blunt.

Horns and spines are found among many other creatures and no doubt help them to survive. One example is the

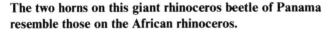

The two horns on this giant rhinoceros beetle of Panama resemble those on the African rhinoceros.

This close-up of a horned toad shows its horns or spines.

horned toad which is not a toad at all but a lizard. These little creatures live in the deserts and desert-like areas of the West and their spiny heads probably protect them from many enemies.

Hairs and scales both grow out of the skin. However, hairs themselves may be spine-like as in the case of the porcupine, which is often called a "quill pig." Most of a porcupine's hairs are stiff, needle-like spines several inches long. They are hard to pull out once they have gotten into an animal's skin. When alarmed, a porcupine turns its back toward the enemy and flips its broad tail into the enemy's face, driving dozens of quills into it.

The African porcupine has even larger quills, some as

long as a foot. They are often sold in fishing tackle stores as floats.

In general, porcupines have few real enemies. Most would-be enemies are quickly discouraged by a face full of quills.

Many other creatures have spines that serve as a means of protection. Some caterpillars have their bodies covered with sharp spines that probably give them protection against birds. Ants found in several parts of the world also have spines. One kind is the leaf-cutting ant found in Louisiana and southward into South America.

The tropical leaf-cutting ant. Note the sharp spines.

The weaver ant, found in some parts of the Tropics, has several hooked spines.

On the coral reefs of tropical beaches live large, slate-pencil sea urchins, whose bodies are covered with heavy spines. Other sea urchins have slender, needle-like spines and some kinds contain poison.

This foot-long slate-pencil sea urchin was photographed on a coral reef of Guam. Its large, heavy spines protect it from many enemies.

5. FLIGHT AND SPEED

Animals have changed in many ways in the millions of years they have been on earth. But no change has made so much difference to their ways of life as the addition of wings. Flight makes it possible for an animal not only to escape from its enemies, but to travel quickly to new food supplies or to warmer climates.

Consider the wild geese and ducks. These birds spend the winter months in warm southern marshlands where food is plentiful and where the water is never frozen. With the arrival of spring they migrate northward for several thousand miles to nest and rear their young. Here there are fewer enemies. Here, too, the water contains a great

Wings enable birds to fly great distances at high speed. These are gulls.

deal of food and the days are long, so they have many hours to feed. Later, after the task of rearing young has been completed, they fly southward down across all of North America. During such flights these geese may fly as fast as 60 miles per hour.

Some birds fly even faster, such as the teal duck and the tiny hummingbird. Yet the teal duck may be captured by falcons flying more than 200 miles per hour.

As far as distance is concerned, the Arctic tern is the champion. It flies southward in winter to southern South America and Antarctica. In spring it returns to the North to nest along the coasts of Alaska, Canada, and Siberia.

Wings have helped birds in another way. Some birds nest high in trees where enemies are few. Ground-nesting birds, such as quail, are at the mercy of such enemies as skunks, rats, foxes, and coyotes.

The Arctic tern is the greatest bird traveler. It nests along the Arctic Sea and then migrates southward.

39

Only a few mammals have the ability to fly. One of these is the flying squirrel. They live in deep forests where they glide from tree to tree. This helps them to escape from enemies and to find food. Their "wings" are really furry skin stretched between their front and back legs. Usually they climb high in a tree, then leap off, sailing away through the forest. They are especially active at night.

Bats are also mammals. When bats long ago changed so that they could fly, they could no longer use their front legs for walking or climbing. The wings of birds and bats take the place of front legs. Of all flying creatures, only the insects have wings that were not legs at one time.

The wing of a bat is made up of thin membranes stretched between the fingers of its front feet.

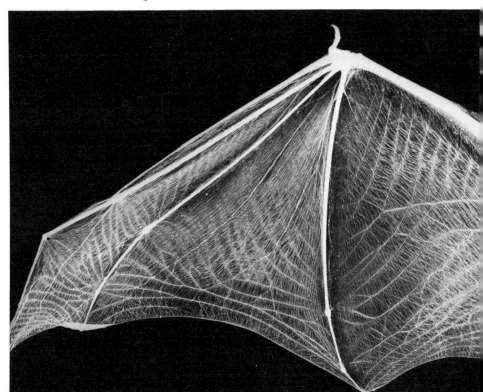

A bat's ears are very large and sensitive.

Bats are creatures of the night, rarely active by day. They flit through the dusk or darkness, guiding themselves and locating flying insects by means of sonar-like senses. While flying a bat emits, or gives off, a series of high-pitched calls which are echoed off of any object in its path. Its highly sensitive ears pick up these echoed sounds and the bat knows at once if a tree limb or a flying moth is in its flight path. This echo-sense enables bats to fly through dense forests and to capture flying insects which are their normal food. Bats thus see with their ears. However, they do have eyes.

41

This large rhinoceros beetle flies with ease, but
its grub-like larva lives in rotting wood.

Insects were the first animals to fly. They took to the air
about 300 million years ago. Wings enable insects to travel
long distances in search of food and homes. Wings enable
the honeybee to fly several miles away from the hive
gathering nectar and pollen from flowers. Scientists have
figured out that in gathering enough nectar to make a
pound of honey, honeybees must fly a distance equal to a
trip around the world. Dragonflies cruise over ponds and
meadows capturing gnats and other flying insects for food.

The dragonfly is one of the most skillful of the flying
insects. Here it is pursuing a mosquito at high speed.

Rabbits have large ears to aid them in escaping enemies. This is a cottontail rabbit.

Speed on the ground is also important to many creatures, especially those that cannot defend themselves. The rabbit is a good example. A cottontail can dart through brush and weeds at great speed and the chances are good that in this way it can get away from its enemies. The jack rabbit is outstanding in its ability to run and dodge. These large rabbits live in open, plains country where there is little vegetation into which they can dart. Yet, by means of their long hind legs, they can hop away at high speed, often at 45 miles per hour, zigzagging in a way that usually saves them from capture by coyotes and foxes.

As a general rule, most defenseless animals living in

43

plains or desert regions have long jumping hind, or back legs, enabling them to dart quickly away from danger. On African deserts there are rat-like jerboas, and on our western plains there are kangaroo rats. Both of these little animals have long jumping legs and are very good at dodging. They are mostly active at night.

Jerboas also live on the large deserts of Arabia. They have long tails tipped with a black and white tuft. When they jump, this tuft bobs up and down on the moonlit desert, probably warning other jerboas that danger is near. The deserts of Arabia also have rabbits or hares that remind us of our jack rabbits and have similar habits.

Great speed is important to many large animals and most of the world's fastest are found in Africa where they must avoid capture by lions and other members of the cat family. The springbok and the pronghorn antelope, for example, have been clocked at 60 miles per hour. However, these animals can be captured by the cheetah when it runs at 70 miles per hour, making it the world's fastest running animal.

Most high-speed animals are of moderate or small size, yet the African elephant can run at 25 miles per hour, while both black and grizzly bears have been clocked at 30 miles per hour. A white-tailed deer can run 40 miles an hour and may jump more than 40 feet.

Great speed to escape from enemies or to obtain food is, thus, important to many animals. It is important whether the animal lives on the ground or flies.

Pronghorn antelope

6. HOMES AND SHELTERS

Many animals build homes as places of safety from enemies. In many cases these homes are used only while rearing young. Examples are coyotes, foxes, and wolves. But many other animals dig holes or dens in the ground and live there all their lives, leaving only to obtain food. Examples are chipmunks, ground squirrels, badgers, and prairie dogs.

A number of insects, too, build snug nests below ground and some kinds live there almost all of their lives. The 17-year cicada lives in the ground for 17 years and then spends only a few weeks in the sun to mate and lay eggs. Many wasps, such as the sphex, dig tunnels in the earth in which young are reared. Horn-worm caterpillars live and feed on plants but, when they are beginning to change into moths, and are helpless, they burrow into the ground where enemies cannot find them. Some other moth caterpillars have this same habit. Ground-nesting ants are common almost everywhere. Some, such as the harvester ants, dig tunnels as deep as 6 feet. Here they are safe from most enemies and from the cold. These ants live on seeds gathered near their tunnels.

Bulldog ants of Australia also nest in the ground. They leave only to capture insect food.

Least expected among creatures that nest in the ground

Harvester ants dig
underground cells where
young are reared and seeds
are stored for food.

A worker bulldog ant rushes out of the underground
nest to drive off an enemy.

**Bank swallows nest in cavities dug
in the banks along streams.**

are certain birds. One of these is the small western
burrowing owl that nests in abandoned prairie-dog burrows.
It feeds on grasshoppers, beetles, and crickets.

Another bird that nests underground is the kingfisher, a
common bird in most parts of the United States.
Kingfishers dig holes in banks near or along streams and
use them as nesting sites. They feed on small fish captured
by diving into the water. There are also bank-nesting
swallows.

Solid or decaying wood, as might be expected, gives
shelter to a large number of creatures. Flickers and most
other woodpeckers use their sharp beaks to chisel nesting

holes in dead trees. In the southwestern United States there are at least two kinds of small owls that use old woodpecker holes in tall cactus plants or in trees as nesting places. These are the pygmy and elf owls.

Early pioneers in America invented the log cabin, but many wild creatures have been building similar structures for millions of years. The beaver is one of the most expert log-cabin builders. It cuts tree limbs of proper length and piles them up into a snug house having a living room inside. These are built either in a pond or alongside a stream. The living room is above the level of the water but it is entered from below. It is hard for an enemy to disturb a beaver's home.

Woodpeckers chisel nesting cavities in dead trees. This is a flicker.

Caddis insects build log-cabin shelters in the water. The larval insect was removed before this picture was taken.

Another clever log-cabin builder is one kind of caddis insect that lives in ponds and streams. During its larval stage it cements small twigs together to form a log-cabin-like structure around itself. It drags this home along with it and, when danger threatens, draws its body inside. Caddis insects of other kinds cement pebbles together instead of twigs. Thus we might say that they were the first carpenters and stonemasons.

Some caddis insects build cases around themselves by cementing small pebbles together.

A number of bees and wasps dig tunnels in hard wood and use these tunnels as nesting places. One of these is the carpenter bee which resembles a bumblebee and is about the same size. With her sharp cutting jaws the female bee cuts deep tunnels in the wood of dead trees. Such a tunnel may be nearly a foot long and about half an inch across. When the tunnel is finished the bee gathers pollen and nectar from flowers and places it at the far end of the tunnel. After a thimbleful of this mixture has been gathered, she lays an egg in it and seals it off. She then stocks more cells and lays an egg in each one. When the eggs hatch the larval bees feed on the mixture of pollen and nectar, well protected from almost all enemies by the hard wooden walls.

As always in Nature there are lazy insects that take advantage of another's labor. Thus it is not surprising to find that certain wasps use old carpenter bee tunnels as ready-made nesting places in which to rear their own young.

The tunnel nest of a carpenter bee dug in solid wood.
Note the mass of pollen and nectar at the far end.
This will serve as food for the larval bee.

Paper nest of bald-faced hornet.

Hornets of several kinds build nests of paper made of wood fiber gathered from weathered posts and dead trees. Some of these paper nests are quite large and are built in trees. Yellowjackets also build paper nests but their nests are underground.

Wasps of many kinds are workers in clay. One of the most skillful of these is the little potter wasp that builds attractive, jug-shaped cells of clay in which its young are reared. These clay pots have narrow necks and flaring tops and the female wasp stocks them with small caterpillars as food for her young.

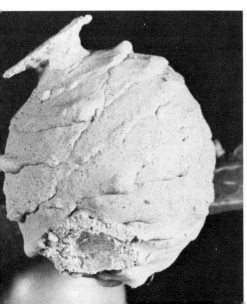

Jug-shaped cell of potter wasp.

52

This mud-dauber wasp has just finished her clay cell.

Also found in most parts of the United States are so-called mud-dauber wasps of which there are two types. Both kinds gather damp clay from the edges of streams or ponds and carry it back to the nest site where it is formed into neat cells in which their young are reared. The clay cells are stocked with paralyzed spiders. One kind of wasp builds separate cells that are about an inch long. However, the female may build several of these cells, all cemented together in a cluster. The other mud-dauber wasp is often called the organ-pipe wasp because she builds her cells in rows, having cross walls between.

Within these hard clay cells the young wasps feed on the paralyzed spiders, safe from most enemies such as birds. Usually the clay cells of mud-daubers are built in locations that are protected from the rain. They are often built on

53

porch ceilings or on the undersides of large rocks extending out from hillsides.

Somewhat similar nest-building habits are found among the cliff swallows. These small swallows gather mud or clay from stream or lake edges and carry it in their beaks to overhanging cliffs where it is formed into neat, gourd-shaped nests attached to the stone. Large numbers of these nests are often built together; sometimes there may be several thousand on the face of a cliff. High on the face of a cliff, these swallows are mostly free of enemies.

Animals build homes of many kinds but there is not enough space to tell about all of them. All these homes help to protect them and their young from enemies. Without such protection these animals could not have survived.

This clay nest under a cliff was built by a western cliff swallow.

54

7. KEEN VISION AND CAMOUFLAGE

The falcon is a hunter, living by capturing and eating other birds. Its eyes are far sharper than those of almost any other creature. Almost like telescopes, they can see details at great distance. Its cousin, the fish hawk, or osprey, is also a sharp-eyed hunter. I have often watched one of these hawks hovering hundreds of feet above a river. Suddenly its wings would close and it would drop like a stone and hit the water, quickly rising again with a trout in its talons.

Sharp vision is almost a necessity to any creature that hunts. This is true of the tiger, the fox, the hawk, or the dragonfly. The eyes of birds are especially adapted for seeing movement and seem to be telescopic, or capable of detecting far-off objects. If we compare the eyes of birds to our own eyes we find several differences. First, a bird's eyeball is flattened and so everything is in focus at the same time. In our case, we focus sharply upon only a small area at a time, and we must move our *eyes* about to see the entire picture. A bird must move its *head* about to look closely at an object. It must cock its head this way and that while examining a bug or a worm. This enables it to judge distance.

The eyes of most birds are located on the sides of their

heads, enabling them to view almost the entire horizon. There are some exceptions to this. Both owls' eyes focus toward the front and so they have *binocular* vision just as we do. In other words, both an owl's eyes can focus on an object at the same time. This is probably an advantage in dim light. It is estimated that an owl's night vision is at least a hundred times better than our own. This enables an owl to fly through dark forests and to see rats and mice upon which it preys.

If you have ever seen an owl in the daytime, you may have noticed that its eyes in the bright light were covered by a thin membrane. This is known as the *nictitating* membrane or "third eyelid." This membrane moves from the inner edge of the eyeball toward the outer edge like a semi-transparent windowshade. It protects the owl's eyes from bright light but also allows it to see during the day.

An owl's eyes are especially adapted for seeing in dim light.

The toad's eyes are very beautiful. The irises are golden. It has keen vision for locating food.

Frogs and toads have excellent eyesight, enabling them to capture insects for food.

Keen vision is also found among many insects, especially those that fly. A dragonfly darts about over a pond seeking mosquitoes and gnats which it captures and eats. This requires acute eyesight. If you could examine a dragonfly's eyes under a hand lens you would find that its eyes are actually made up of thousands of individual eyes. This is the type of eyes found in almost all insects. Each of these "eyes" sees one small portion of the visual field. Such insects are said to have *compound* vision. This type of eye is especially effective in seeing moving objects.

Under a lens you can also see that the individual facets on the upper portion of a dragonfly's eyes are larger than those on the lower portion. There is a reason for this. A dragonfly approaches its flying prey from below, spotting it in the large upper facets or individual "eyes" which are fitted for distant vision. When close to its prey, the dragonfly then sees it through its lower, smaller "eyes" which are especially fitted for nearby vision. Many horseflies have similar eyes and these insects might be said to have *bifocal* vision.

A dragonfly has the keenest vision of any insect. Each eye is made up of thousands of individual eyes or facets. The upper facets are larger, fitted for distant vision.

In this close-up photo it can be seen that each eye of a whirligig beetle is divided. One eye sees above the water's surface and the other sees below.

As we have seen, most creatures that prey upon others have keen vision. This is true also of such insects as mantises, robber flies, and hunting wasps. There are, however, some interesting exceptions. Take the army ants of the tropics, for example. These ants are among the world's most voracious hunters and yet they are blind. Apparently they depend upon other senses in locating their prey.

An unusual case is that of the gyrinid beetles, sometimes called whirligig beetles. These black beetles are often seen swimming rapidly about on the surfaces of ponds or pools. They have, of course, many enemies both above and below the water's surface. In order to see these enemies, whirligig beetles have divided eyes. That is, each eye has one portion fitted for seeing above the water and the other portion fitted for seeing below.

Since the animal world has many hunters it is not surprising that many of the hunted have developed ways of outwitting them. This enables the plant-eaters to survive.

Some animals escape their enemies by speed, but others do so by means of camouflage. That is, they are colored or marked in ways to make them invisible or to look like something else. Some tree frogs are colored to resemble the lichen-covered bark of trees on which they usually rest. The

This tree frog is marked and colored to resemble the lichen-covered bark of trees on which it usually rests.

Find the butterfly. When this butterfly closes its wings and alights among dead leaves, it is difficult for a bird to see it.

under surfaces of some butterfly wings mimic dead leaves. When they alight and fold their wings they are difficult to see. Many tree-dwelling insects, such as katydids, are green, making them hard to see among the leaves. The walking stick insect has a very slender body and when it rests on a twig is difficult to find. (See picture, next page.) Many caterpillars use this same trick.

61

The walking-stick insect escapes the keen eyes of birds by resembling a twig. It lives in trees.

In the tide pools of tropical coral reefs I saw small fish that I decided to call dead-leaf fish because that is exactly what they looked like. They drifted about in the current, rarely swimming as most fish do. They were colored and marked like dead leaves. It was only by accident that I discovered that they were actually fish. When I tried to pick up one of these "dead leaves," it darted away, much to my surprise.

This book has told of some of the ways by which the world's animals survive. Each one survives because it can, in some way, protect itself from enemies or can capture its food.

62

INDEX

Numbers in italics indicate illustrations

63